GRIME'S GRA

NORFOLK

Peter Topping

Grime's Graves is one of only ten flint mines recognised so far in England. Dating from roughly 3000–2000BC, it spans the later Neolithic and the beginning of the Early Bronze Age periods. The Anglo-Saxons thought this pockmarked landscape was the work of the god Grim, but excavations have shown that it was in fact man-made, and represents some of the earliest evidence of mining in the country. The mines were dug by prehistoric men to extract the underlying layers of high-quality flint required for axes and other tools.

A tour of Grime's Graves is a unique experience: it is the only flint mine in the UK that allows the visitor to enter the underground galleries where Neolithic miners once worked. The presence of the mines, and later land use, have also shaped the natural history of the site which is recognised as a Site of Special Scientific Interest (SSSI).

❖ CONTENTS ❖

Grime's Graves
Lynford, Thetford, Norfolk IP26 5DE
Tel. 01842 810656
Visit our website at www.english-heritage.org.uk

Published by English Heritage
1 Waterhouse Square, 138-142 Holborn, London EC1N 2ST
Copyright © English Heritage 2003
First published by English Heritage 2003
Reprinted 2005, 2007, 2009
Unless otherwise stated, all photographs are © English Heritage.

Editor: Louise Wilson. Design: Pauline Hull. Plan: Richard Morris.
Production: Elaine Pooke.
English Heritage photography by Steve Cole and Alun Bull unless otherwise stated.

Printed in England by the colourhouse
ISBN 978-1-85074-852-6
04962   C50   05/09

Mixed Sources
Product group from well-managed
forests and other controlled sources
www.fsc.org Cert no. SGS-COC-2524
© 1996 Forest Stewardship Council

FSC

TOUR

The place name Grime's Graves is Anglo-Saxon in origin, deriving from the pagan god Grim and meaning 'Grim's quarries' or the 'Devil's holes'. Clearly the Saxons had some notion of what the site might have been, but in later times Camden (1695) thought it was 'small trenches and ancient fortifications' and Blomefield (1805) a 'Danish encampment'.

Grime's Graves is one of England's earliest mining sites: the first pits opened over 5000 years ago. The site lies in the Norfolk Breckland ('breck' land was the local name for temporary fields), an area of rolling heathland that includes a dry valley leading up to the gentle domed chalk ridge where the mines are located.

A recent survey has found that Grime's Graves was one of only ten

The Breckland heaths of Grime's Graves seen at sunrise

Neolithic flint mines recognised in England, and of these, only six now survive as earthworks. The mounds and hollows visible at Grime's Graves cover 7.6 hectares, representing 433 mineshafts, pits, quarries and spoil dumps. To date, at least 28 mines have been excavated. Further evidence of mining may be buried by sand blows or levelled by later ploughing around the edges of the site. Although large, Grime's Graves is not the biggest flint mine in England: Martin's Clump and Stoke Down (both in southern England) are more extensive, but in comparison with some European mines such as Krzemionki (Poland) or Jablines (France) they are all relatively small.

Flint mining in England first started on the South Downs at the beginning of the Neolithic period around 4500BC. However, the mines at Grime's Graves did not come into use until much later, the first pits being dug around 3000BC and the last about 2000BC. Mining at Grime's Graves is therefore broadly contemporary with the building of much of Stonehenge.

Flint is one of the hardest rocks, and appears to have been formed from silica and marine sediments. It is usually found in flat sheets or seams of irregular nodules, and was valued by prehistoric man for tool-making because of its fine flaking qualities. The distinctive seam of black flint found in the Brandon area and known as 'floorstone' by the gunflint knappers was also much prized by the British army for its sparking qualities when used in flintlock muskets.

The presence of the Neolithic mines, and later land use at Grime's Graves, have shaped the natural history of the site which is recognised as a Site of Special Scientific Interest (SSSI). Plants like the Rock Rose and Heath Bedstraw grow freely, and wildlife such as the common lizard, various butterflies, skylarks, wood-peckers and nightjars all visit the site. There are also several bat roosts.

Stonehenge in Wiltshire. Many of the massive stones here have evidence of mortice and tenon joints, exactly the type of jointing used by woodworkers who may have used flint axes like those produced at Grime's Graves. The later stones at Stonehenge, therefore, seem to have followed an earlier tradition using the construction techniques of timber-built circles

ENGLISH HERITAGE/JAMES O. DAVIES

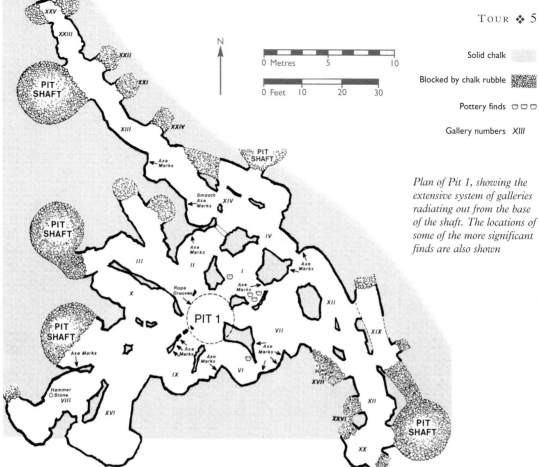

N

| 0 Metres | 5 | 10 |

| 0 Feet | 10 | 20 | 30 |

Solid chalk

Blocked by chalk rubble

Pottery finds

Gallery numbers   *XIII*

Plan of Pit 1, showing the extensive system of galleries radiating out from the base of the shaft. The locations of some of the more significant finds are also shown

PIT 1

This is the only flint mine in the UK currently open to visitors; access is through a small green building near the visitor centre and down a ladder.

Pit 1 was excavated in 1914 by A. E. Peake. Excavating down through the shaft fills, three layers of flint were discovered, the 'topstone' at 3m, the 'wallstone' at 7m and the 'floorstone' at 9m in depth. The shaft was surrounded by a spoil dump, and was almost 10m wide at its mouth, reducing to 3.6m at the bottom of the shaft. The backfilling of the shaft had been done in stages, and five hearths or fireplaces were found at intervals between 3m depth and the floor of the shaft. Clearly the miners had lit fires periodically during the backfilling, perhaps as some form of

The ladder descending into Pit 1

Right: One of two later Neolithic Grooved Ware bowls discovered during the 1971 excavations lying on a chalk platform at the bottom of a shaft. With only internal decoration, this type of pottery is very rare

commemoration or dedication, or during feasting (some animal bones were also discovered).

At the base of the shaft six galleries had been dug, radiating outwards to follow the jet-black floorstone flint sought by the miners. These galleries linked through to five adjacent shafts, and produced a wide range of finds. Rope marks were found above the entrance to gallery II; numerous antler picks were left scattered about the workings; the remains of a red deer were discovered in gallery XV; and three different species of bats were recorded. The fact that bats were found demonstrates that some mines were quiet and open long enough for roosts to become established – they were not quickly backfilled. Fragments of later Neolithic Grooved Ware pottery were recovered alongside flint implements and carved chalk 'cups' and balls. Many of these artefacts are not mining tools, and must indicate that other activities took place during mining.

PIT 2

Pit 2 lies on the western side of the minefield, midway between the visitor centre and the site boundary. It is now heavily eroded.

This flint mine was also excavated by A. E. Peake between 1914 and 1915 and re-opened by the British Museum in 1975. Here the topstone lay at 4m depth, the wallstone at 7m and the floorstone at 9m. As in Pit 1, a number of hearths were found throughout the fill of the shaft, again suggesting fires lit as part of a ritualised closing of the mine. Many layers also produced animal bones, indicating feasting or offerings placed in the mineshaft. Halfway down the shaft, a female skeleton was found, but this was not a deliberate burial.

At the base of the shaft lay a hearth, and a chalk and sand platform abutted the north-east wall.

Neolithic miners at work. Excavations have found evidence for timber platforms built across the width of the shafts to ease the hauling of the nodules. Recent information from Fengate, near Peterborough, suggests that notched tree trunks may have been the norm for the ladders. (Reconstruction by Terry Ball)

On the shaft wall near the platform, a series of vertical incised lines was found by archaeologists and interpreted as a sundial as it was lit by the sun's rays at midday. A second graffito – a lattice design – was found on another part of the shaft wall, and thought to be tally marks scratched by the miners as they counted flint nodules.

The red deer antler pick was the favoured tool of the Neolithic miners at Grime's Graves. Many of the picks found during recent excavations have been discovered to have a covering of chalky clay in which were imprinted the palms and fingerprints of the Neolithic miners

Ten galleries opened out from the base of the shaft and, unusually, marks from a polished stone axe were found cut into their walls. However, the main mining tool was the antler pick, and many of these were found scattered throughout the mine. Later Neolithic Grooved Ware pottery was found in various galleries and at the base of the shaft; several galleries produced remains of bats. Taken together, this evidence again suggests that pottery, feasting or offerings of meat joints and graffiti all played a part in mining.

The geology at Grime's Graves is known as the 'Brandon Flint Series', characterised by three distinctive flint layers lying below sands and clays and interspersed between chalk. It was the lowest layer, known as floorstone, which was generally targeted by the Neolithic miners because it was easily flaked and had a lustrous deep black colour.

The available radiocarbon dates suggest that mining took place over a period of roughly 1000 years. The fact that there were some 500 mines suggests that they were dug at intervals of one to two years. Mining was not intensive nor on an industrial scale as we understand the term.

At Grime's Graves the Neolithic miners dug mines up to 13m deep with radiating galleries and shallower pits from 3m to 8m deep. The galleries range from 0.6m to 1.5m in

MINING TECHNIQUES ❖

height and width. The smaller pits lie on the northern and western slopes, while the deep mines cluster on the higher ground to the south. The mines have occasionally been grouped together with two or three in a single quarry: some quarries contain up to ten shafts, suggesting that certain mines were dug in sequence.

Excavations in 1971 discovered that a turf wall held back the sandy soils around the shaft. Surface earthworks also record mining waste dumped between the shafts, piled perilously on narrow ridges of land. However, once mining had cleared the base of the shaft and the first gallery, rubble from subsequent galleries was dumped in the old workings to avoid lifting it to the surface.

The main mining tool was the red deer antler pick, although two ground stone axes have been found. Once at the flint layer, the miners prised up the nodules from the floors of the galleries and shaft. Nodules may have been raised up the shafts in rope-hauled baskets (from the evidence of rope marks in Pit 1), and platforms were built into some shafts to help stage the lifting process.

It is clear that the miners carried out a number of rituals during mining. In 1971 two highly decorated pots were discovered on a chalk platform; Pit 15 produced seven antler picks on another platform; and many mines had 'cups', balls, phalli and other objects carved from chalk. Hearths which were not used for lighting or cooking were found on the floors of many shafts. Numerous animal remains, perhaps offerings, have been found, and in Greenwell's Pit a dog had been placed in one of the galleries. These examples suggest that ceremonies took place in the mines, possibly to ensure plentiful supplies of flint and the safety of the miners.

Above and bottom left: The two Grooved Ware bowls found during the 1971 excavations

Below: The excavation of Pit 1 in 1914, showing some of the antler picks discovered in the mine

The excavations of Pit 2 in 1914. Note the windlass used to haul up the excavated chalk from within the mine

A view inside Greenwell's Pit, showing some of the galleries radiating out from the base of the shaft

The earthworks surrounding Pit 2 tell an interesting story of the 1914–15 excavations. On the north-eastern side, a narrow cut can be seen through the lip of the shaft, which was the barrow run leading from the dig into the adjacent shaft where the dig spoil dump can be seen. On the south-western side there is a second excavation spoil dump partly filling another shaft.

GREENWELL'S PIT

This mine lies in the south-eastern part of the site near the southern boundary and now has a concrete cover.

Canon Greenwell partly excavated this flint mine between 1868 and 1870, encountering the topstone flint at 4m, the wallstone at 8.7m and the floorstone at a depth of 12m.

Although these were not the first excavations at a flint mine, they were the first to identify correctly the date and purpose of such sites. Consequently this flint mine has an important place in the history of archaeological research. The mine was re-opened and further excavated by the British Museum between 1974 and 1976.

Greenwell discovered numerous antler picks scattered throughout the mine, but also a ground stone axe made of greenstone from Cornwall. This axe was found in a gallery where marks from its blade were cut into the walls. It was lying on the ground, placed below two parallel antler picks with their tines facing inwards; between these was the skull of a phalarope, a rare shore bird. Clearly this was not an accidentally dropped group of finds – Grime's Graves is a long way from the sea and the wading bird would not have lived nearby. It seems rather to have been a setting of important artefacts (both the skull and axe brought from some distance), probably put there by the miners when the gallery had been worked out. The skeleton of a dog was found in another gallery by the British Museum.

Neolithic Grooved Ware pottery, cups, a phallus of carved chalk and evidence of at least one episode of flint knapping were all recovered from this mine.

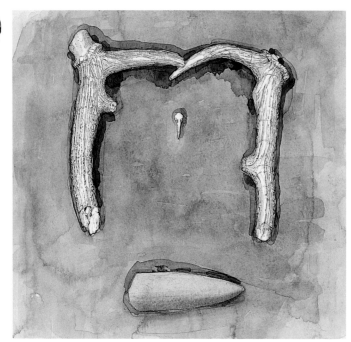

PIT 15

Pit 15 lies 30m to the north-east of the visitor centre and is now covered by a concrete cap.

Leslie Armstrong excavated this flint mine in 1937–9 and discovered the topstone flint at a depth of 2m,

Above: A reconstruction of the setting of antler picks, greenstone axe (bottom) and phalarope skull (centre) found in a gallery of Greenwell's Pit. Above left: A phalarope skull. The phalarope (left) is a shorebird which is now a rare visitor to the coasts of Britain. Although its Neolithic distribution is uncertain, the nearest stretch of coast to Grime's Graves, now some 75km (46.5 miles) to the east, was even further away in Neolithic times, so the skull was brought from some distance. (Illustrations by Judith Dobie)

WHAT WAS PRODUCED AT GRIME'S GRAVES?

Right: The tools of the flint knapper. Nodules were broken down into smaller pieces using hard stone hammers, and worked into finished artefacts with softer antler or bone tools

One of the questions raised by Grime's Graves is why the miners dug for flint, when adequate surface deposits were available around the site. One argument is that better quality flint came from the deep layers, particularly for making large tools such as axes. However, during the preceding Mesolithic period, outcropping flint was used to manufacture large tools such as tranchet axes and 'Thames picks'. Big artefacts did not need mined flint. The fact that the miners went to a lot of trouble to dig the mines, in a small-scale and carefully focused way, and carried out a range of rituals in the mines, all suggests that mined flint had a special value to the Neolithic communities and had to be dug out in a particular way. This value was then further enhanced when the flint was crafted into certain types of tools. Many axes, for example, were never used and were placed in 'hoards', suggesting a ceremonial use

Neolithic miners at work in a gallery. Chalk blocks are being prised from the walls, while another miner shovels up the rubble using an ox shoulder blade. Note the polished axe lying on the floor: such axes appear to have been used to mark the gallery walls in a few parts of the mines. (Illustration by Judith Dobie)

The chalk 'goddess' discovered during the excavations in 1939. The authenticity of this carving has always been disputed

rather than a functional one. Perhaps they symbolised the role axes played in clearing the forests to establish the new farming way of life introduced during the Neolithic period.

When the flint nodules were raised to the surface they were knapped, on 'working floors', into rough shapes, some becoming finished tools (many rough-outs were traded and finished elsewhere). Axes and discoidal knives were two of the main tools made at Grime's Graves, but relatively large numbers of cutting flakes, points and scrapers were also found, which suggests that there was an emphasis on cutting in the Late Neolithic tool kit at the site. By contrast, the later Middle Bronze Age flints from Grime's Graves, made from recycled flint, featured tools for piercing, so there was clearly a change of emphasis in the use of flint tools between these periods.

the wallstone at 4.5m and the floorstone at 6m. Nine galleries radiated out from the base of the shaft.

The excavation of this flint mine was one of the most controversial at Grime's Graves, particularly concerning the discovery of 'Palaeolithic' artefacts, notably the chalk 'goddess', claimed by Armstrong to prove that mining pre-dated the Neolithic period. This figurine, however, together with dubious Palaeolithic-style etchings found in 1921, while they did echo the style of earlier Palaeolithic carvings, were all greeted sceptically: the weight of evidence argued for a Neolithic date. Armstrong held firmly to his beliefs, but this proved to be his last excavation at Grime's Graves.

Leslie Armstrong (centre) excavating at Grime's Graves during the 1930s

HISTORY

Grime's Graves is not a site that dates from one single period. It has a long history and many other periods are represented here, although often in very subtle ways.

THE NEOLITHIC BACKGROUND (*c.*4500–2000 BC)

The Neolithic period was one of dynamic change. During the preceding Mesolithic period people led a mobile existence, living off the land and following the seasonal movements of wild animals and the availability of plants and berries. However, by roughly 4500 BC, a number of significant changes had taken place in Britain that completely altered the pattern of life in a number of ways.

It was during the early Neolithic period that people first built enclosures, typically with many entrances or 'causeways', and used them for a variety of special events. Unusually, permanent settlements were few, perhaps reflecting the fact that people continued to move around the landscape and only met each other at the enclosures for seasonal ceremonies. It is also at this time that large burial monuments – long barrows and chambered tombs – were first built, to house the dead in chambers of timber or stone.

A significant feature of the Neolithic period was the introduction of farming techniques, including both the cultivation of cereals and the domestication of animals. It appears that this lifestyle change was introduced gradually over many centuries before it had a significant impact upon the landscape. Initially hunting and gathering continued alongside farming, and it was not until later in the Neolithic period that field systems became more established.

Technological changes were also taking place. Pottery was introduced,

Opposite: A small encampment of miners at Grime's Graves. The archaeological evidence suggests that perhaps no more than one mine was open at any one time. The reconstruction portrays an earlier mine still being commemorated by the setting of a fire in the disused shaft a short distance from the current mine. Again, this is an event recorded by the archaeological evidence. (Illustration by Judith Dobie)

Below: The earlier Neolithic period witnessed the transition from a hunting and gathering lifestyle towards a growing reliance on farming, until by the end of the period and into the Bronze Age settled farms became more commonplace. (Illustration by Judith Dobie)

and stone tools were now ground into more regular, smoothed shapes which improved their tensile strength and aesthetic qualities. Set against this backdrop of major changes in the ways people lived in, viewed and used the landscape, flint mining began on the rolling chalk downlands of south-eastern England. These flint mines were used intermittently for almost 1500 years, although not all at once nor any of them for this full length of

Left: The first really significant inroads into the woodland canopy happened during the Neolithic period. (Illustration by Peter Dunn)

time. In contrast to the mines, special types of stone were also quarried from the axe 'factories', many near mountaintops such as Langdale in Cumbria and Graig Lwyd in Gwynedd.

By roughly 3000BC the earliest flint mines and enclosures were being abandoned at a time when new types of communal monuments were being built – the large circular enclosures known as henges and the enigmatic stone and timber circles. The first

Below: A timeline for the Neolithic flint mines at Grime's Graves, based upon calibrated radiocarbon dates. (Illustrated by Judith Dobie)

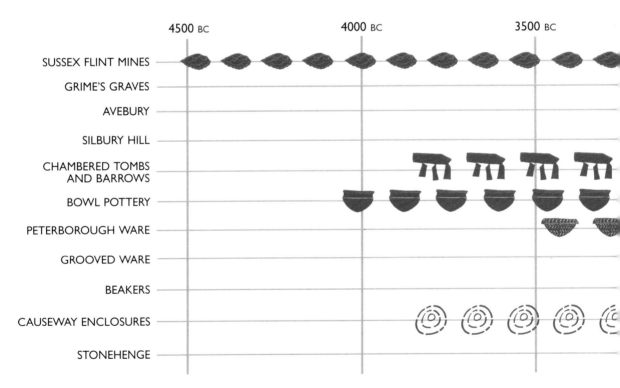

parts of Stonehenge were constructed, but flint mining was not forgotten and the first pits and shafts at Grime's Graves were opened. Although there may have been some overlap with the end of mining in the south, at Grime's Graves a new focus had developed and continued for some thousand years, actually coinciding in the last centuries with the introduction of the first metal tools made of copper after *c.*2500BC. By the time the massive stone trilithons were being erected at Stonehenge to create the monument we know today, flint mining at Grime's Graves was coming to an end.

Above: Stonehenge as it would have appeared when mining was coming to an end at Grime's Graves. (Reconstruction by William Brouard)

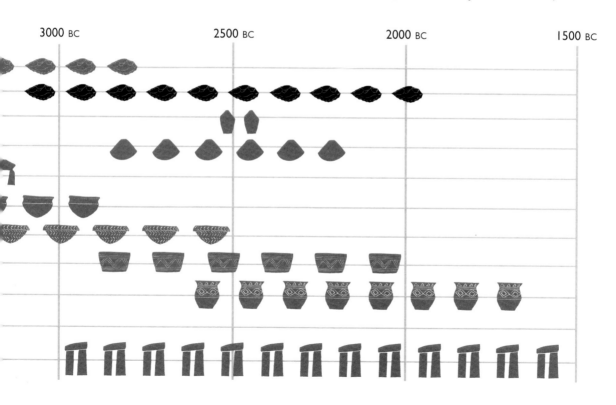

During the Bronze Age the first really settled farms and field systems appeared in the British countryside, although hunting and gathering still played a role. (Illustration by Judith Dobie)

THE BRONZE AGE (*c.*2300–800 BC)

Very little Early Bronze Age activity appears to have occurred at Grime's Graves: only a few fragments of pot of this date have been found. However, by the Middle Bronze Age, *c.*1500–1150 BC, there is an explosion of settlement evidence, but perversely without the sites of any houses being found. What has been discovered is massive midden or rubbish deposits dumped into a number of the Neolithic mineshafts. Over 8000 pottery fragments have been found of so-called Deverel–Rimbury ware, evidence for metalworking, together with some 6 tonnes of worked flint, making this the largest group of artefacts of this date in the UK. Clearly such an accumulation of rubbish would have taken some time to develop. These middens also produced evidence of textile production, leather and wood working and pottery manufacture. Animal bones from cattle, sheep or goats, pigs, horse and deer, suggest both meat consumption and dairy production. Seeds of wheat and barley were also found,

providing evidence of crop cultivation.

It seems that the Middle Bronze Age community that lived at Grime's Graves was able to produce much of the food it needed and many of the artefacts it required. Although no houses have been found here, this is not unusual. At Mildenhall Fen, 15 kilometres to the south-west, two similar middens were excavated, again without any obvious settlement evidence being found. Perhaps Middle Bronze Age houses left little trace for archaeologists – unless they are looking in the wrong places.

THE IRON AGE (*c.*800 BC–AD 43)

During the Iron Age people continued to visit Grime's Graves. Several excavations have produced pottery sherds of this date, although no settlements have yet been found. The most significant discoveries came from the upper fills of the mineshaft excavated in 1971 where two inhumation burials were uncovered. These had been buried in sequence. The first burial was of a young adult woman with a decorated chalk plaque by her hip; the second, which partly destroyed the first, was of an adult male with a necklace (or earrings) comprising two iron beads. Both burials appear to have involved ceremonies including setting fires and the placing of offerings. It is possible

Right: The medieval Warren Lodge at nearby Thetford, used by the warrener as a base from which to protect the commercial rabbit farms

that other skeletons found in the upper fills of mineshafts during earlier excavations may be Iron Age in date. These burials seem to fit a regional tradition in southern and eastern England for re-using pits.

LATER HISTORY

Although there does not seem to have been significant activity at Grime's Graves during the Roman period (AD43–410), Roman pottery sherds have been found. These span the first to late fourth centuries AD, and are from pots manufactured in Gaul, Spain, Oxfordshire, the Lower Nene Valley and probably East Anglia. The sherds are weathered, which suggests that they may have been brought to the site during or after the Roman period, though it is not known why.

The pagan Anglo-Saxons gave names to both the site and Grimshoe mound (Grim's Howe, meaning Grim's, or Woden's, burial mound) on the eastern edge of the minefield. This mound later gave its name to the administrative unit known as the hundred and became its meeting place during the earlier medieval period. The Brecks were the least settled area of East Anglia at the time of the Domesday Book (1086), but from the twelfth

ENGLISH HERITAGE/JONATHAN BAILEY

century onwards rabbit warrens were created. These proved successful, even during the plague years (1348 onwards). From 1224 Grime's Graves appears to have been owned by Bromehill Priory who probably used it as a warren – the site was all but surrounded by rabbit warrens at this time. However, by the sixteenth century Grime's Graves had become sheep pasture.

A map of 1761 shows not only a very early plan of Grime's Graves but also, in the West Field, a number of 'breaklands of the Lord of the Manor', recording typical Breckland temporary fields near the mines. Faint traces of this cultivation can still be seen.

In about 1820 coniferous woodland was planted over the mines, and was well established by the time a sketch was made in *c*.1850 by the Reverend Luke from nearby Weeting. As recently as 1905 the Ordnance Survey map still depicted

Below: An illustration from the fourteenth-century Luttrell Psalter showing a 'pillow mound' – such mounds were built by warreners as artificial homes for rabbits

THE BRITISH LIBRARY/HERITAGE IMAGES

the west field as a mixture of arable and pastureland.

EXCAVATIONS AT GRIME'S GRAVES

The first excavations at Grime's Graves took place in 1852 when the Reverend Pettigrew dug two pits and Reverend Manning separately opened others. In 1866 the Reverend Manning returned and excavated further pits. All of these early digs are poorly recorded.

Perhaps the most significant excavations at Grime's Graves occurred in 1868–70 when Canon Greenwell was able to demonstrate – for the first time anywhere in Britain – that flint mines were prehistoric in date. Greenwell discovered the existence of deep shaft and gallery mining; he also identified the red deer antler as the main mining tool, and from the discovery of a stone axe in one of the galleries deduced that the mines were Neolithic in date.

The earliest known sketch of a flint mine: a charcoal and pencil drawing of Grime's Graves dating from c.1850, by the Reverend G. V. Luke from the nearby village of Weeting in Norfolk

❖   # LATER USES

Flint has had a number of uses since the Neolithic flint mines were abandoned. The widespread availability of flint has led to its use in many buildings in East Anglia. The Romans built their fort at Burgh Castle with flint and brick walls which still stand 4.5m high. Grand buildings such as Long Melford church in Suffolk – largely fifteenth-century, and built in part with Brandon flint – and Weeting Castle, a twelfth-century Norman fortress 4km to the west of Grime's Graves, show the variety of buildings constructed using flint.

From the fourteenth century onwards, flint was used in 'flushwork', where nodules were knapped into a variety of shapes to create patterns. It was not only the grand buildings which were decorated with flushwork:

Brandon has examples of fine hand-shaped oval flushwork in the walls of several nineteenth-century houses on London Road. Brandon's flint knappers were responsible for the flintwork on many East Anglian churches, and the flint chips from their other main industry – gunflint knapping – were used for building foundations.

The invention of the flintlock gun in c.1600 led to the development of the gunflint industry, and Brandon became one of its major centres from 1790 onwards because of the high quality of 'Brandon Black' flint. The demand for gunflints grew from 360,000 per month in 1804 to over 1 million per month by the end of the Napoleonic Wars in 1813. Despite a

Below left: A detail of the oval-shaped flint flushwork used in the frontage of a nineteenth-century house in Brandon

Below right: This nineteenth-century detached house in Brandon is a fine example of domestic flint architecture

OF FLINT ❖

slump following the end of hostilities, the Brandon knappers continued to supply building flint, the East India Company exported their gunflints, and by 1868 they were producing 23 different types of gunflints for markets in Asia, Africa and South America.

Many of the gunflint workshops were located in Thetford Road, run by families such as the Fields, Edwards, Carters and Snares. From 1810 onwards Lingheath, on the south-eastern side of Brandon, became the main flint mining area, although others existed at nearby Weeting, and Santon Downham. However, all of these mines had been abandoned by the 1930s.

The modern flint miners worked alone, using a one-sided pick (in shape like the Neolithic antler picks), crowbar and shovel, to dig a stepped shaft. Each step was roughly at shoulder height to allow the miner easily to lift the nodules onto it and thus gradually raise them step by step up to the surface. Lighting was by candles, which were also used to time the working day when they had burnt down.

With the death of the last knapper, Mr Fred Avery, in 1996, it may be that the Brandon gunflint industry has finally died out.

CHRIS LUCAS COLLECTION

Above: Gunflint knappers 'quartering' a nodule at Fred Snare's workshop in Brandon in the early twentieth century

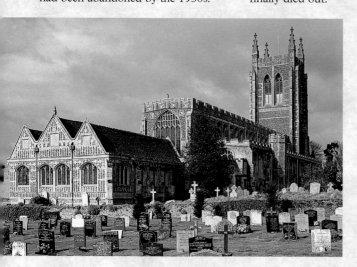

Left: Long Melford church, Suffolk, one of the greatest achievements in the architectural use of flint. Although what survives of the church is mostly fifteenth-century, the tower was rebuilt between 1898 and 1903 with flint flushwork from Brandon and Acton
Below: A detail of the flint flushwork and ashlar tracery in the church tower

No further excavation occurred here until 1914, following erroneous suggestions that flint mining was Palaeolithic in date, and thus much earlier than the Neolithic period. Subsequently, a number of individuals, notably Leslie Armstrong, tried to prove a Palaeolithic date, despite a paper written in 1933 which had conclusively demonstrated the Neolithic date of all flint mines. Armstrong did make notable discoveries: he found considerable evidence for later Bronze Age activity, and that mining had covered a much larger area than represented by the earthworks. However, much of his evidence for Palaeolithic mining is now widely considered to have been part of a hoax, perpetrators unknown.

Excavations by Roger Mercer in 1971–2 on behalf of the Department of the Environment, and then between 1972 and 1976 by the British Museum, have ensured that Grime's Graves remains the most widely explored and best-known flint mine in England.

Grime's Graves came into public ownership in 1931 from the Forestry Commission. In 1985, because of its special Breckland flora and fauna, the site became classified as a Site of Special Scientific Interest (SSSI).

The excavations at Pit 1 in 1914. At this time there were still many mature trees covering the site, most planted a century earlier

NATURAL HISTORY
OF GRIME'S GRAVES

Breckland lies in south-west Norfolk and north-west Suffolk. It is an important wildlife habitat which stretches from Swaffham in the north to near Bury St Edmunds in the south. It is an area of light soils, of low rainfall (the average is less than 560mm or 22in a year) and of relatively extreme temperatures. The underlying rock is chalk but this is covered by sands, gravels and tills which are the result of glacial activity during the Ice Age. The weathering of these glacial deposits has produced a number of soil types which vary from the very alkaline to the highly acid. Before the arrival of the first farmers, this area, like much of Britain, was covered with forest. In the area of Grime's Graves the main trees were lime, oak and hazel. During the Neolithic and Bronze Age, patches of forest were cleared to provide small arable fields, probably on the more fertile chalky soils. It was not until the Iron Age, perhaps around 500BC, that widespread forest

clearance took place and the characteristic Breckland heaths developed, with heather dominant on the acid soils and with grassland on the more alkaline soils. Cereals were grown, but the thin soils and low rainfall meant that yields were usually lower than on clay or peat.

In the Middle Ages the term 'breck' was used for fields which were cultivated for a short period and

The landscape of Grime's Graves today

ALAN WILLIAMS/NHPA

Skylarks are regular
visitors to Grime's Graves

then left fallow for a number of years. The area was named Breckland by W. G. Clarke in 1894. In the Middle Ages much of the area was used for grazing sheep and farming rabbits in warrens. Although the farming of rabbits continued at Lakenheath until the twentieth century, many escaped to live wild. Grazing, particularly by rabbits and sheep, was responsible for maintaining large areas of open heathland with distinctive flora and fauna found nowhere else in Britain. In places there was overgrazing and the light sandy soils would blow across the countryside engulfing buildings, as in 1668, when part of Santon Downham was overwhelmed by sand which had blown 8km (5 miles) from Lakenheath Warren. During the Napoleonic Wars of the late eighteenth and early nineteenth centuries more land was ploughed up, and pine shelter belts were planted to prevent sand blows. Some of these still exist. However, later in the nineteenth century, farm profits fell and it became increasingly difficult for Breckland farmers to make a living. In 1922 the Forestry Commission began to plant conifers and now over 200 square kilometres have been established. Little of the Breckland heathland survives, except in the Ministry of Defence Stanford Training Area (not open to the public) and a number of designated nature reserves. During the twentieth century the Breckland heathland

decreased from 7000ha to 2900ha.

The natural history of Grime's Graves is of considerable interest and importance, and is often directly related to land use. The site is officially listed as a Site of Special Scientific Interest. Pit 15, which is no longer open to the public, is an important winter roost for rare bats, particularly Natterer's and Daubenton's, two of the species which used the mines as a winter roost during the Neolithic period. Canon Greenwell's Pit, reopened in 1974–6, is also a winter bat roost. Visitors can occasionally see roe deer, which live in the surrounding forest (red deer live elsewhere in Breckland), grey squirrels and rabbits. In spring many skylarks are heard singing as they soar upwards. Kestrels are seen hovering over the site, while jays and woodpeckers can be heard, and sometimes seen, in the nearby woodland. Occasional flocks of crossbills fly over the site and, on summer evenings, nightjars can be heard churring on the adjacent heath.

The soils vary across the site: acid soils overlie the sands while alkaline, chalky soils cover the upcast from the mineshafts. Because of this the area supports a wide range of interesting plants. The influence of soil upon the vegetation is particularly striking on the north side of the dry valley, outside the English Heritage area. Many visitors have asked about these stripes, formed by alternating bands of dark and light vegetation. They look as if they were deliberately planted, but are in fact the result of soil disturbance by periglacial action during the Last Glaciation, more than 10,000 years ago. The soil under the dark stripes is particularly acid and is covered with heather. The soil under the lighter stripes is less acid and covered in grass.

In the English Heritage site where the sandy acid soil is relatively undisturbed, particularly near the entrance to the site and at the far (southern) end, grasses are dominant, particularly Bent grass (*Agrostis species*) and Sheep's Fescue (*Festuca ovina*).

Good management of this important site for wildlife is essential. Without continued grazing the heathland at Grime's Graves would soon be colonised by scrub and woodland, and the special plants and animals of the more open habitats would be lost. Rabbits continue to graze and burrow on parts of the site, maintaining a short turf and bare areas which provide a suitable habitat for many low-growing plants, especially annuals. Grime's Graves is also grazed by Norfolk Wildlife Trust's flock of native sheep, which are well adapted to grazing the rough grasses of the Breckland heaths. Together the sheep and rabbits maintain the heath much as it has been for hundreds of years. In

places, scrub and bracken have escaped the attention of the grazing animals, and some of this is cleared to prevent gradual encroachment on the heath.

Other plants can also be found here, particularly Heath Bedstraw (*Galium saxatile*), a low mat-forming plant with small white flowers from June to August, and the Many-headed Woodrush (*Luzula multiflora*), with grass-like leaves fringed with long hairs and rush-like flowers in May–June. In the areas not grazed by sheep the grass grows long and is tussocky, and bracken, small shrubs and trees, such as hawthorn and pine, can be found. The plants in the area of the deep shafts are much more varied. Some of the plants, such as Woodsage (*Teucrium scorodonia*), Thale Cress (*Arabidopsis thaliana*) and the rare Spring Vetch (*Vicia lathyroides*) are more commonly found on acid soils, while others, such as the purple Wild Thyme (*Thimus drucei*) and the yellow Rock Rose (*Helianthemum chaemaecistus*) are usually found on chalk soils. Many of the plants found in this area are low-growing, such as the yellow Bird's-foot Trefoil

A Cinnabar caterpillar feasting at Grime's Graves

Below: Some of the wildflowers that can be seen at Grime's Graves (from left): Breckland Wild Thyme, which has pinkish-purple flowers (June–September); the rare Purple Milk-vetch, which flowers May–September; and the colourful yellow and violet Breckland Pansy (April–October). (Drawings by Judith Dobie)

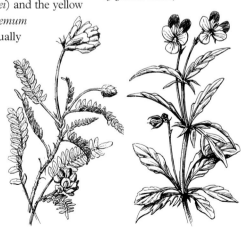

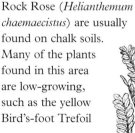

(*Lotus corniculatus*), rare Purple Milk-vetch (*Astragalus danicus*) and white-flowered Field Mouse-ear (*Cerastium arvense*). Among the taller plants are the purple Giant Knapweed (*Centaurea scabiosa*), the yellow Dark Mullein (*Verbascum nigrum*) and the Spiny Restharrow (*Ononis spinosa*), with its red pea flowers. This is a particularly interesting area as the plant communities of acid and chalky soils merge into one another.

Right: In late spring the yellow Rock Rose carpets Grime's Graves, dramatically picking out the undulations of the earthworks

FURTHER READING

M. Barber, D. Field and P. Topping, *The Neolithic Flint Mines of England*, English Heritage, Swindon, 1999

M. Barber, D. Field and P. Topping, *Grime's Graves, Norfolk*, NMR Report TL88 NW4, RCHME, Swindon, 2000 [unpublished archive report]

J. Clutton-Brock, *Excavations at Grimes Graves, Norfolk, 1972–1976, Fascicule 1: Neolithic Antler Picks from Grimes Graves, Norfolk, and Durrington Walls, Wiltshire: A Biometrical Analysis*, British Museum Press, London, 1984

S. Hart, *Flint Architecture of East Anglia*, Giles de la Mare Publishers Ltd, London, 2000

A. J. Forrest, *Masters of Flint*, Terence Dalton Ltd, Lavenham, 1983

A. J. Legge, *Excavations at Grimes Graves, Norfolk, 1972–1976, Fascicule 4: Animals, Environment and the Bronze Age Economy*, British Museum Press, London, 1992

I. Longworth, A. Ellison and V. Rigby, *Excavations at Grimes Graves, Norfolk, 1972–1976, Fascicule 2: The Neolithic, Bronze Age and Later Pottery*, British Museum Press, London, 1988

I. Longworth, A. Herne, G. Varndell and S. Needham, *Excavations at Grimes Graves, Norfolk, 1972–1976, Fascicule 3: Shaft X: Bronze Age Flint, Chalk and Metal Working*, British Museum Press, London, 1991

I. Longworth and G. Varndell, *Excavations at Grimes Graves, Norfolk, 1972–1976, Fascicule 5: Mining in the Deeper Mines*, British Museum Press, London, 1996

R. J. Mercer, *Grimes Graves, Norfolk, Excavations 1971–72, volume I*, HMSO, London, 1981 [Department of the Environment Archaeological Reports No. 11]

R. J. Mercer, *Grimes Graves, Norfolk, Excavations 1971–72, volume II: The Flint Assemblage by A. Saville*, HMSO, London, 1981 [Department of the Environment Archaeological Reports No. 11]

T. Pearson, *Lingheath Farm, Brandon, Suffolk*, NMR Report TL78 NE81, RCHME, Swindon, 1996 [unpublished archive report]

ACKNOWLEDGEMENTS

English Heritage would like to thank the following organisations and individuals: the staff of the British Museum, particularly Gill Varndell, for their assistance with the preparation of this guidebook, and the Trustees for kind permission to reproduce the photographs held in the museum; the Norfolk Record Office, for granting permission to reproduce the sketch by the Reverend Luke; Chris Lucas, who provided unpublished photographs of the gunflint industry in Brandon; English Heritage staff photographers Steve Cole and Alun Bull, who took the majority of the photographs reproduced here; and Martyn Barber and David Field, who undertook the original survey of Grime's Graves with the present author. To all go sincere thanks.